PLAY BALLADS

With A Band

Music Minus One

8063

SUGGESTIONS FOR USING THIS MMO EDITION

WE HAVE TRIED to create a product that will provide you an easy way to learn and perform these compositions with a full ensemble in the comfort of your own home. The following MMO features and techniques will help you maximize the effectiveness of the MMO practice and performance system:

Because it involves a fixed accompaniment performance, there is an inherent lack of flexibility in tempo. We have observed generally accepted tempi, and always in the originally intended key, but some may wish to perform at a different tempo, or to slow down or speed up the accompaniment for practice purposes; or to alter the piece to a more comfortable key. You can purchase from MMO specialized CD players & recorders which allow variable speed while maintaining proper pitch, and vice versa. This is an indispensable tool for the serious musician and you may wish to look into purchasing this useful piece of equipment for full enjoyment of all your MMO editions.

We want to provide you with the most useful practice and performance accompaniments possible. If you have any suggestions for improving the MMO system, please feel free to contact us. You can reach us by e-mail at *info@musicminusone.com.*

Music Minus One

8063

contents

WITCHCRAFT

Cy Coleman and Carolyn Leigh

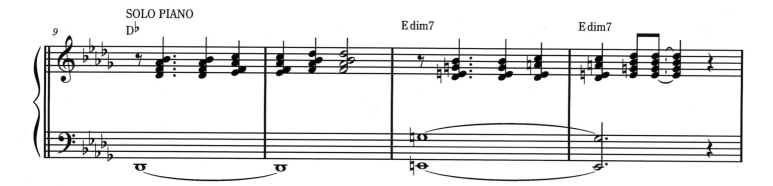

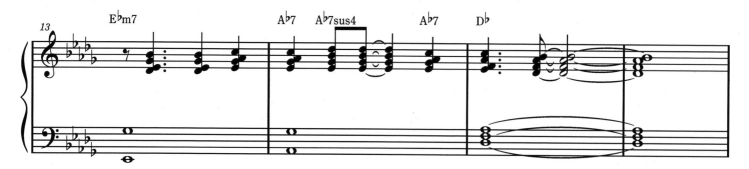

Witchcraft
Music by Cy Coleman
Lyrics by Carolyn Leigh
© 1957 MORLEY MUSIC CO.

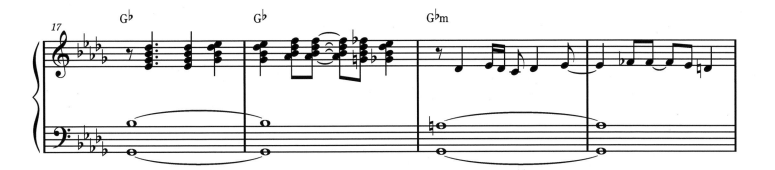

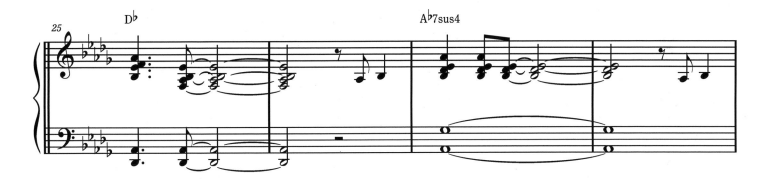

6

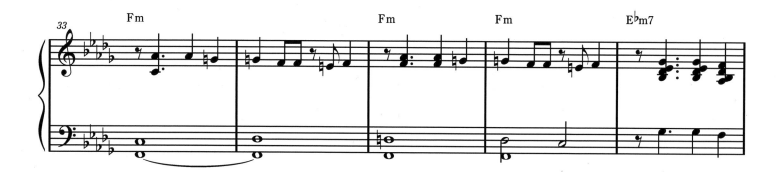

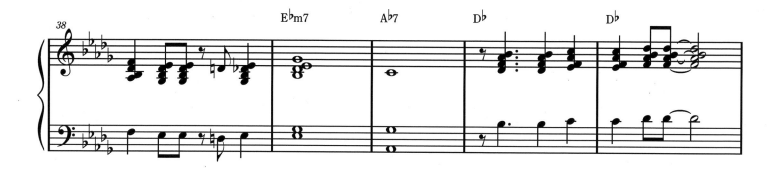

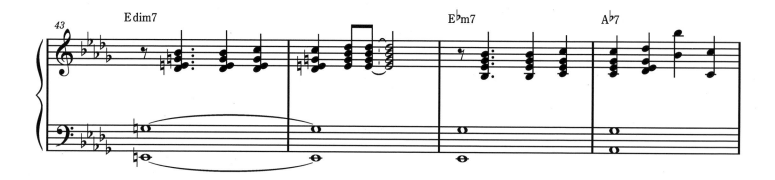

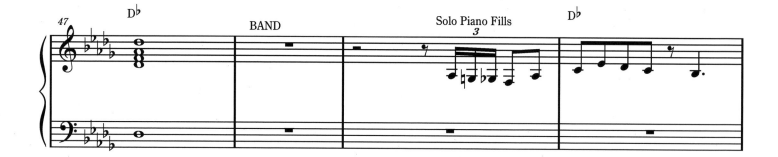

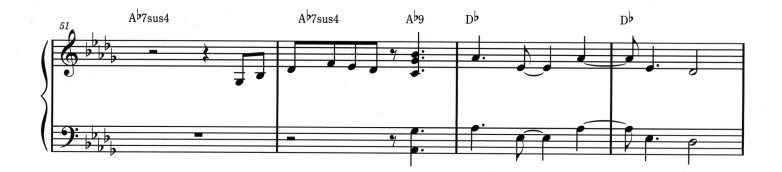

MMO 8063

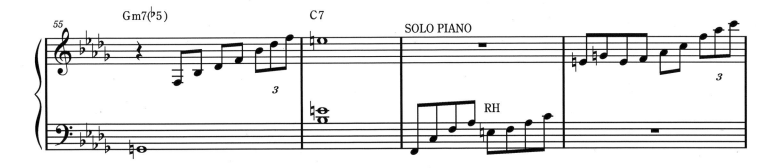

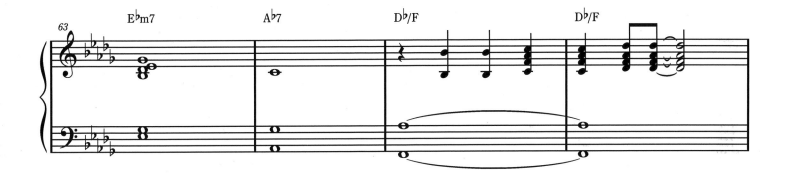

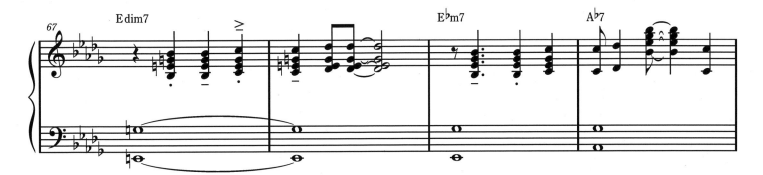

ONE FOR MY BABY

Harold Arlen and Johnny Mercer

One For My Baby (And One More For The Road)
from the Motion Picture THE SKY'S THE LIMIT
Lyric by Johnny Mercer
Music by Harold Arlen

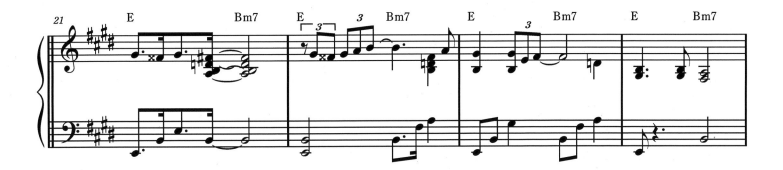

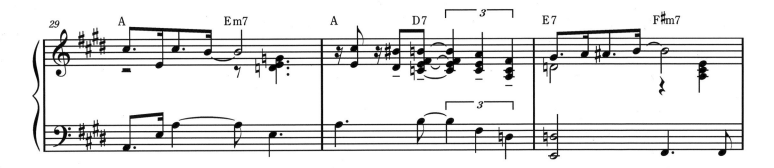

MMO 8063

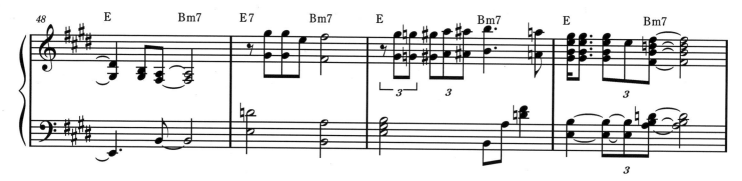

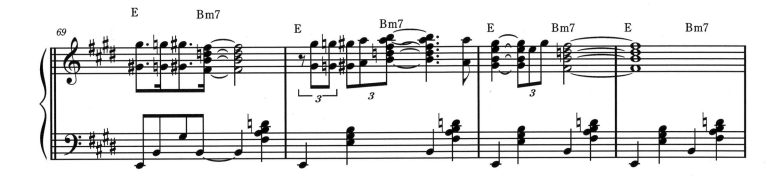

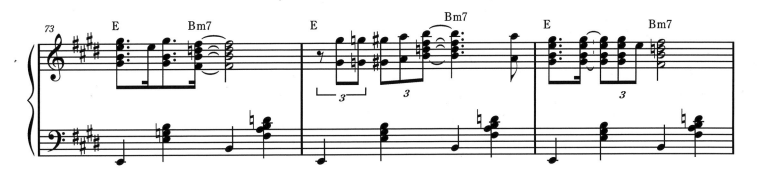

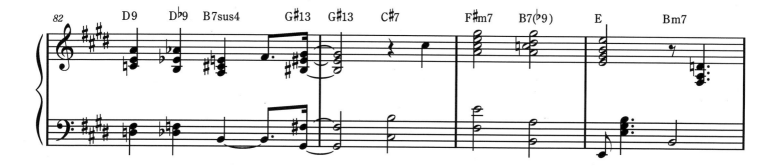

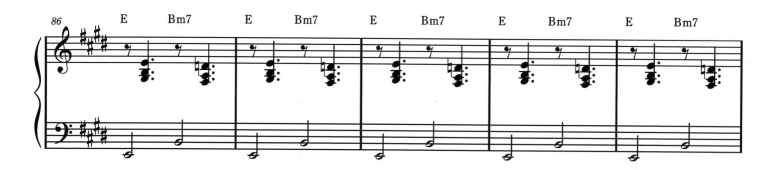

PLAY WITH TRACK UNTIL FADEOUT

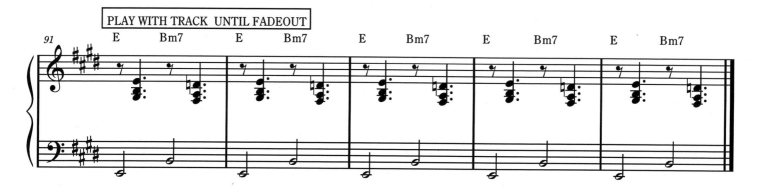

MMO 8063

TENDERLY

Walter Gross and Jack Lawrence

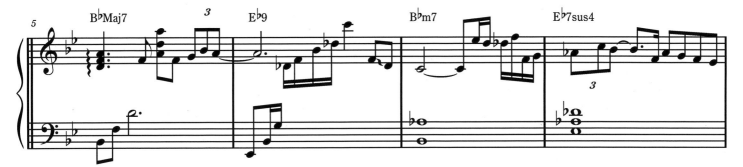

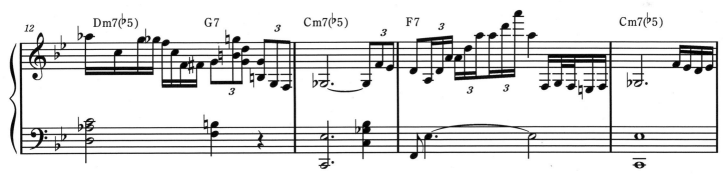

Tenderly
from TORCH SONG
Lyric by Jack Lawrence
Music by Walter Gross

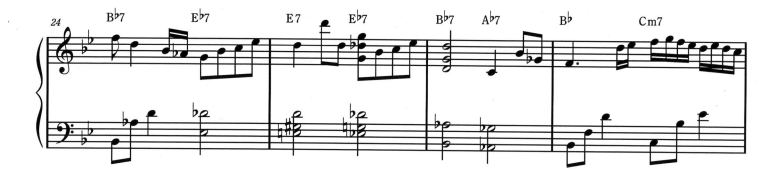

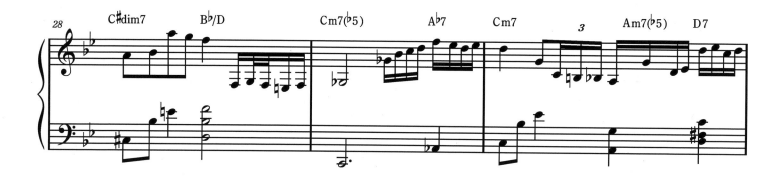

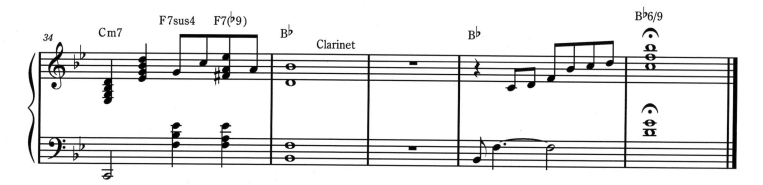

THE CHRISTMAS SONG

Mel Torme and Robert Wells

SOLO PIANO

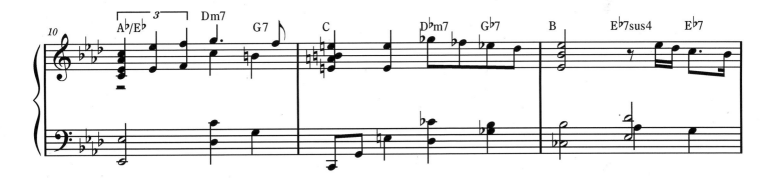

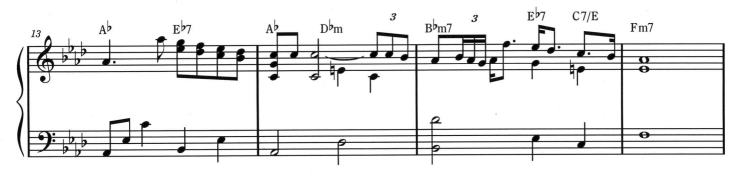

The Christmas Song (Chestnuts Roasting On An Open Fire)
Music and Lyric by Mel Torme and Robert Wells

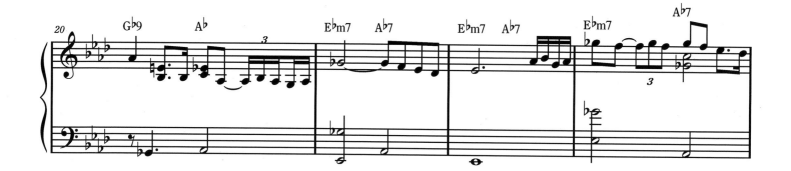

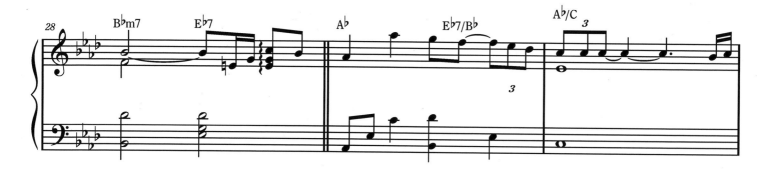

Play this behind clarinet

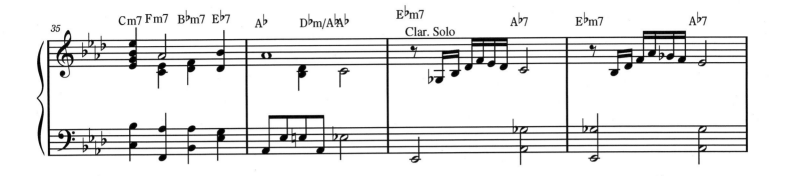

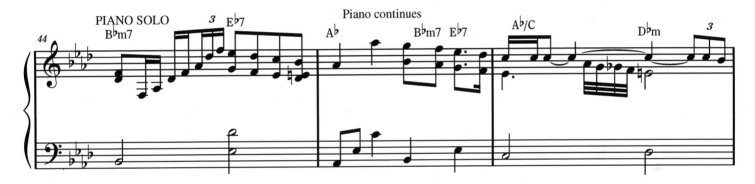

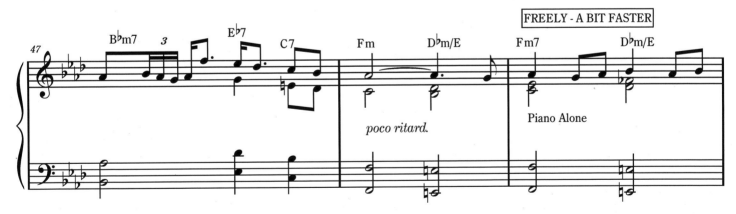

AFTER YOU'VE GONE

Turner Layton and Henry Creamer

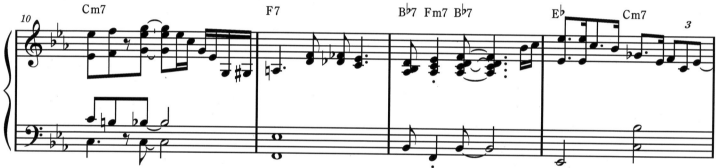

After You've Gone
Music by Turner Layton
Lyrics by Henry Creamer
© 2009 RAMAPO Music Co. (BMI)
This arrangement © 2009 Ramapo Music Co. (BMI)
All Rights Reserved   Used by Permission

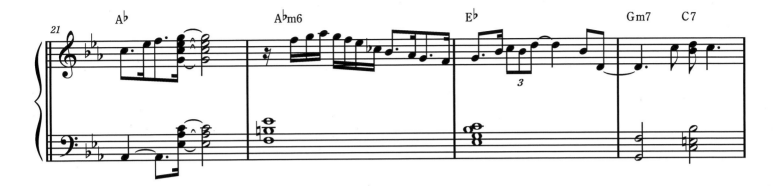

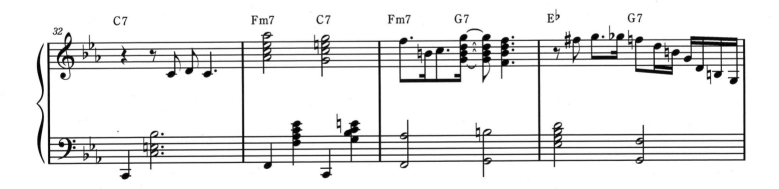

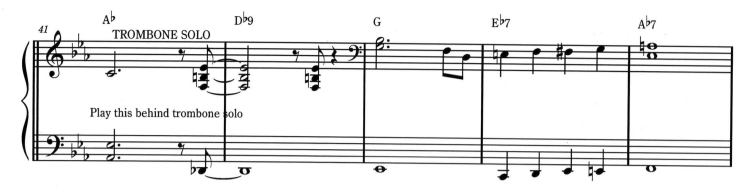

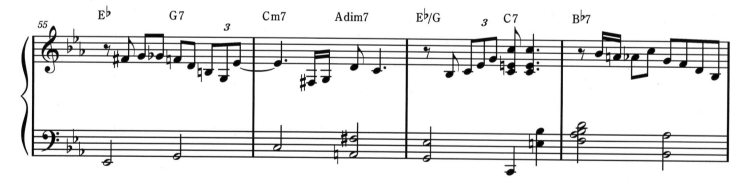

MANHATTAN

Richard Rodgers and Lorenz Hart

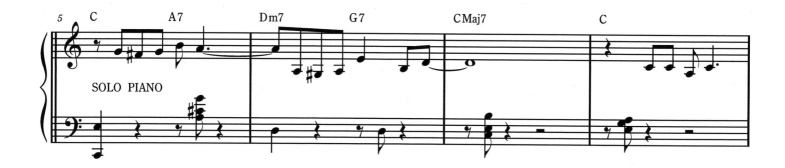

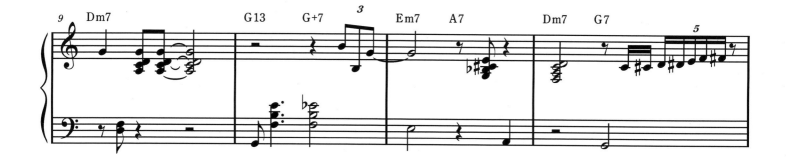

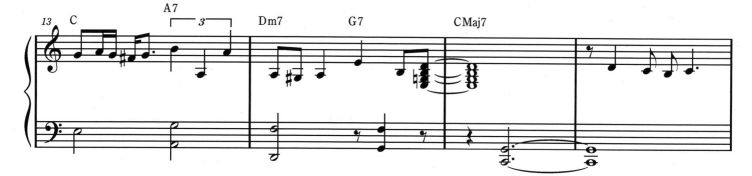

Manhattan
from the Broadway Musical THE GARRICK GAIETIES
Words by Lorenz Hart
Music by Richard Rodgers

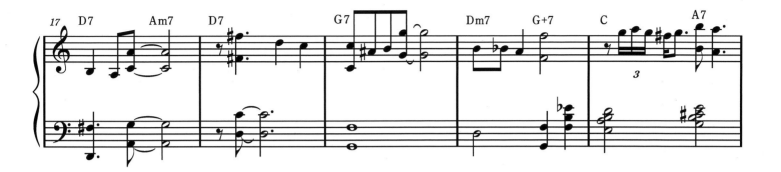

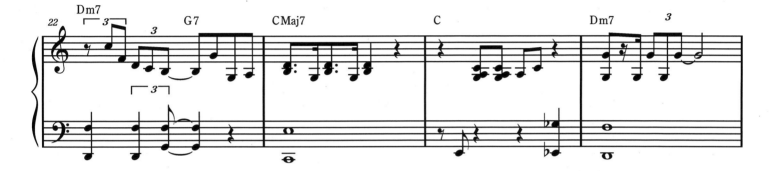

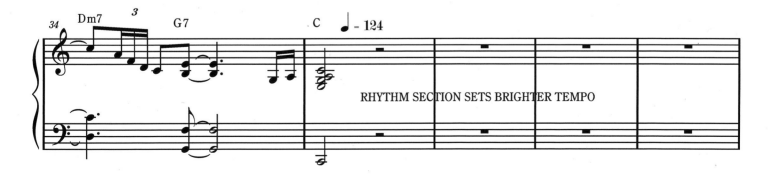

RHYTHM SECTION SETS BRIGHTER TEMPO

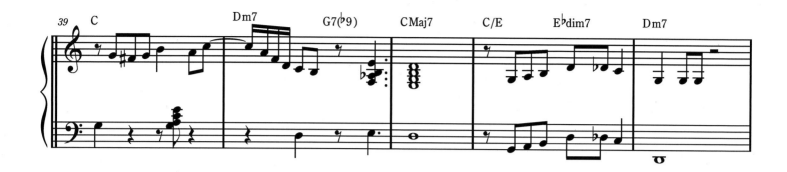

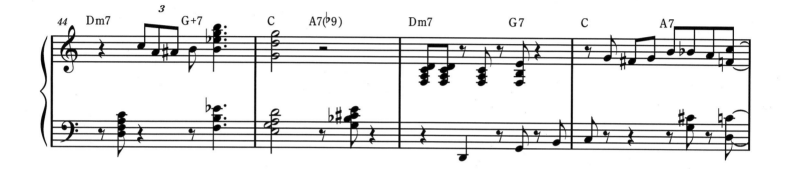

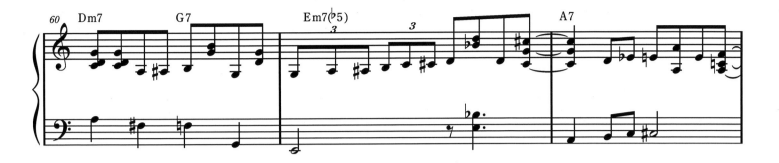

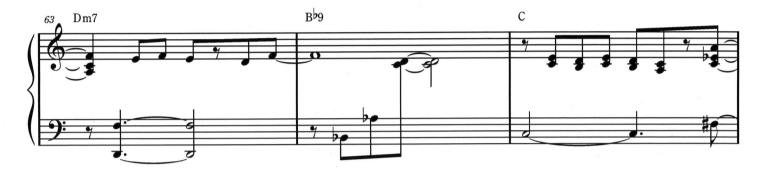

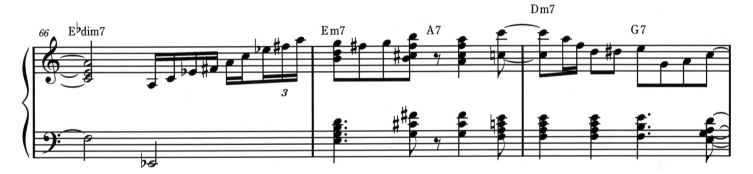

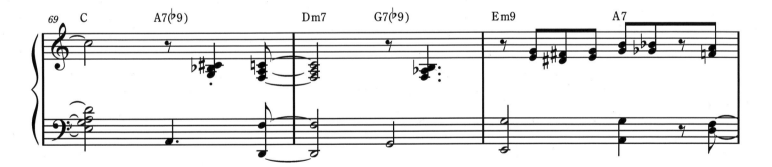

WHY DON'T YOU DO RIGHT

Joe McCoy

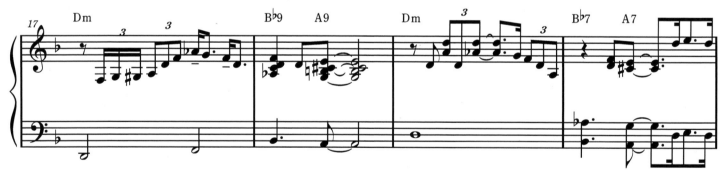

Why Don't You Do Right (Get Me Some Money, Too!)
By Joe McCoy
© 1941, 1942 EDWIN H. MORRIS & COMPANY, A Division of MPL Music Publishing, Inc.
© Renewed 1969, 1970 MORLEY MUSIC CO.
This arrangement © 2008 MORLEY MUSIC CO.
All Rights Reserved   Used by Permission

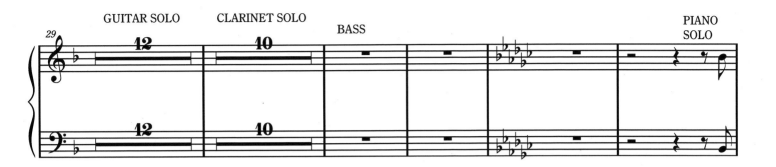

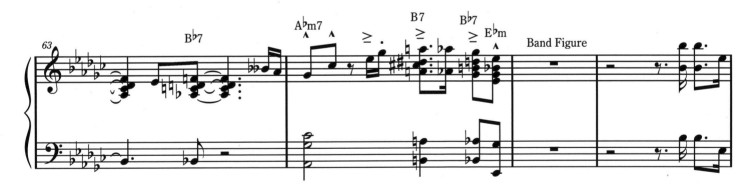

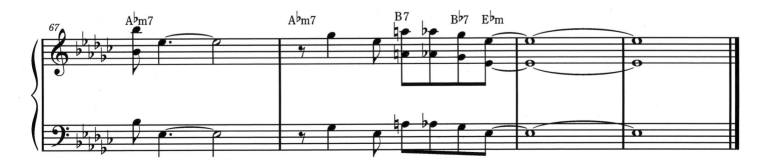

I'M GLAD THERE IS YOU

Paul Madeira and Jimmy Dorsey

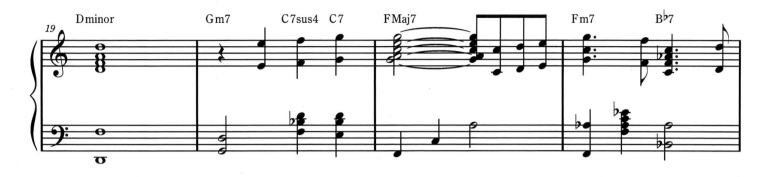

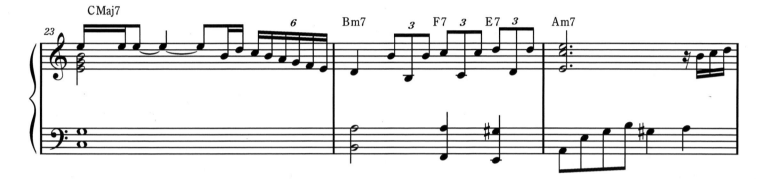

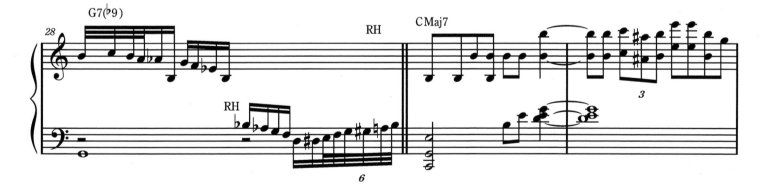

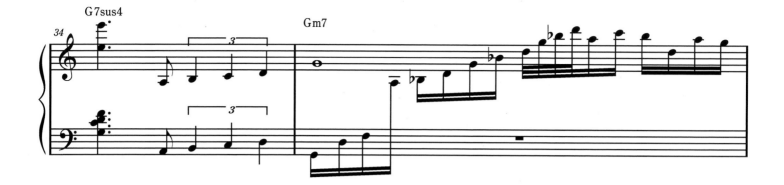

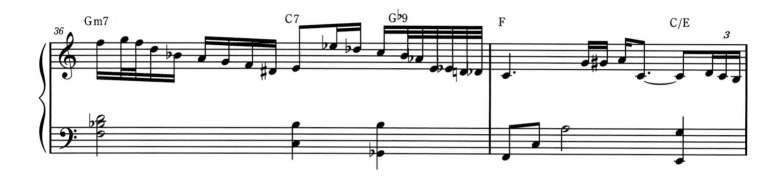

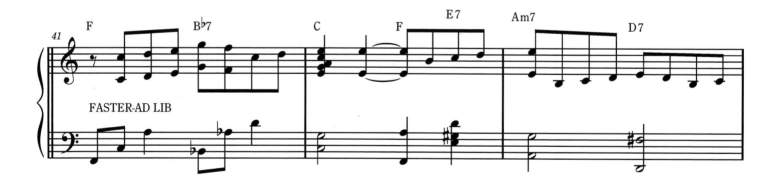

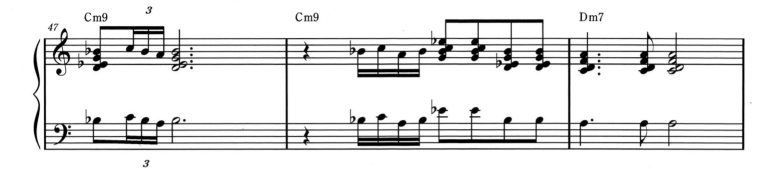

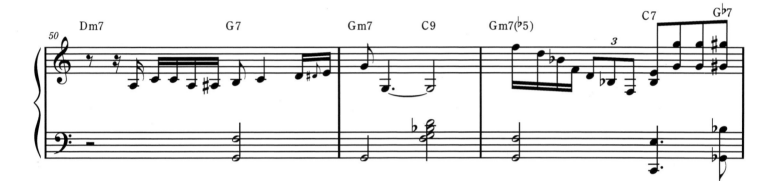

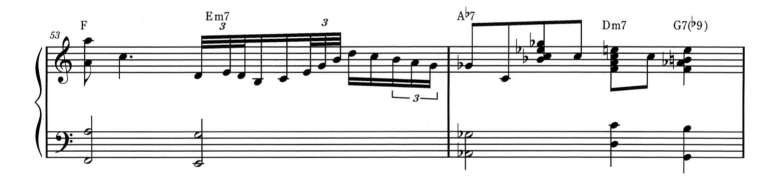

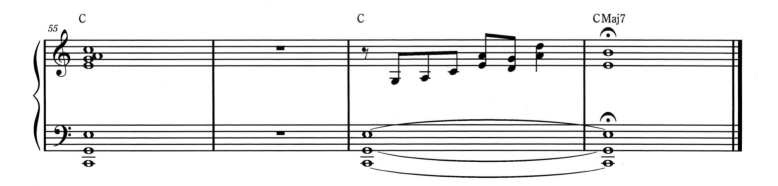

WHAT A DIFF'RENCE A DAY MADE

Maria Grever and Stanley Adams

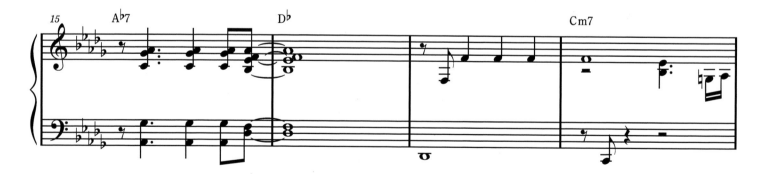

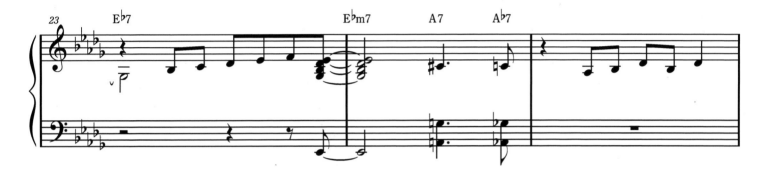

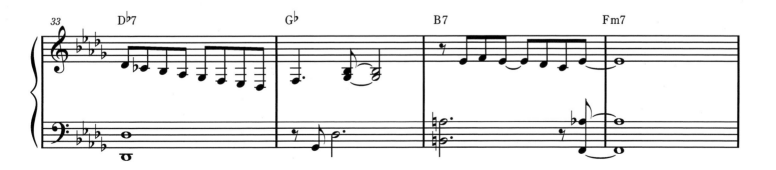

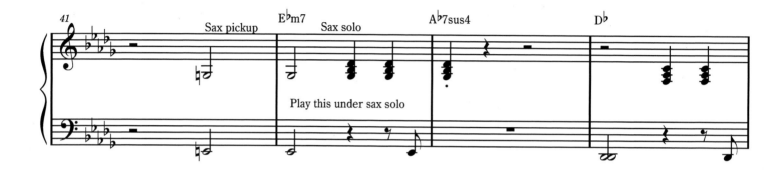

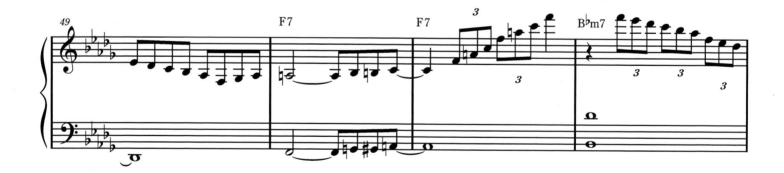

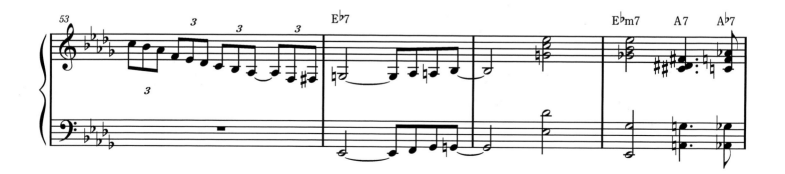

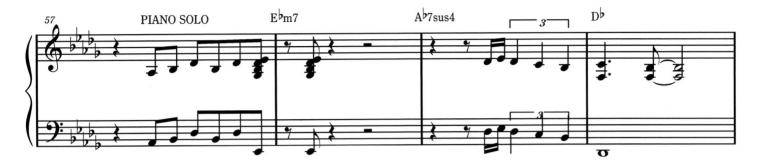

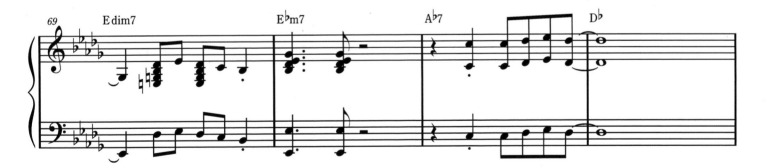

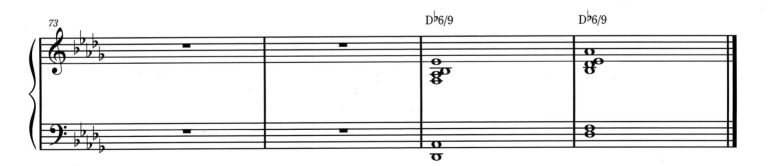

SENTIMENTAL JOURNEY

Bud Green, Les Brown and Ben Homer

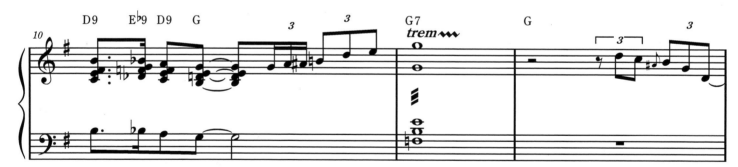

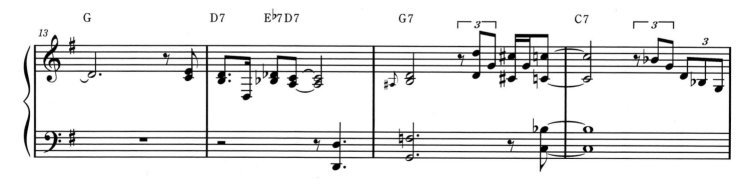

Sentimental Journey
Words and Music by Bud Green, Les Brown and Ben Homer
© 1944 (Renewed) MORLEY MUSIC CO. and HOLLIDAY PUBLISHING
This arrangement © 2008 MORELY MUSIC CO. and HOLLIDAY PUBLISHING
All Rights Reserved   Used by Permission

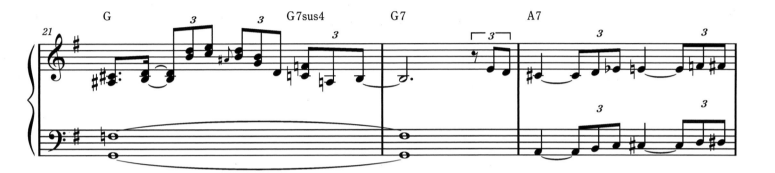

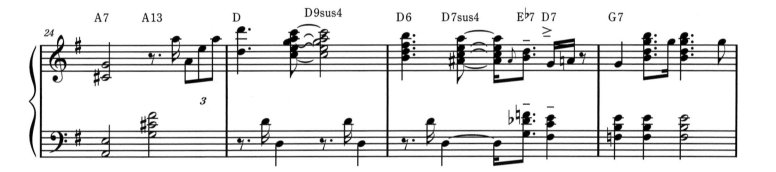

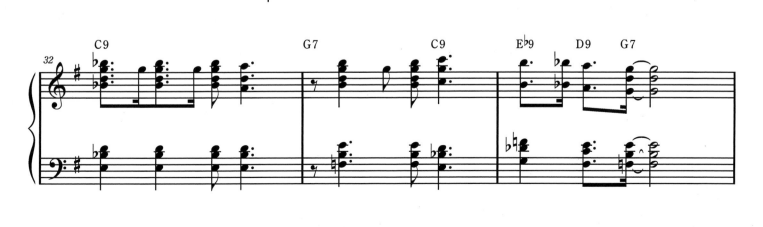

TROMBONE SOLO   CLARINET SOLO   SOLO PIANO   C

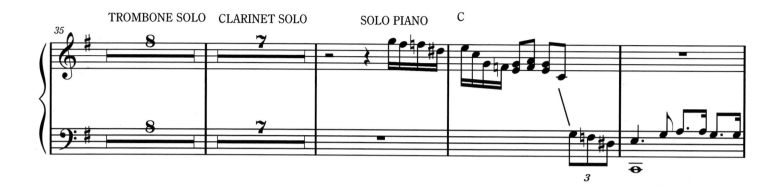

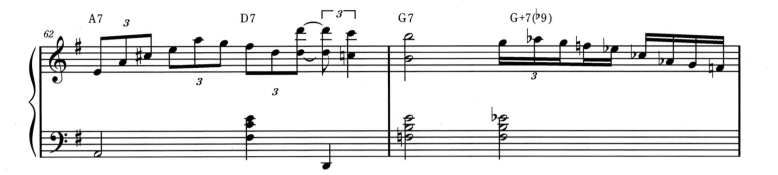

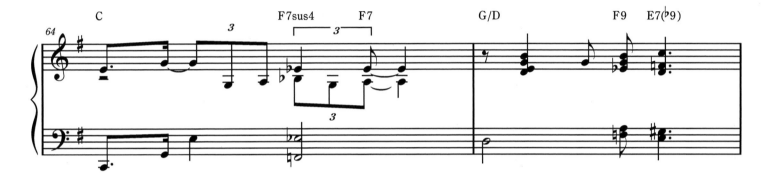

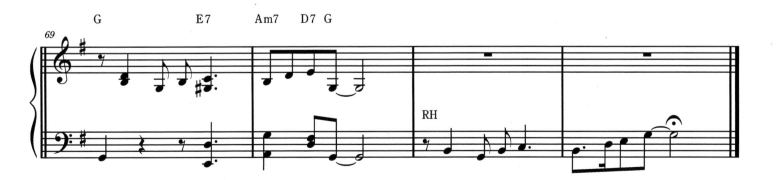

MUSIC MINUS ONE
50 Executive Boulevard
Elmsford, New York 10523-1325
800-669-7464 (U.S.)/914-592-1188 (International)

www.musicminusone.com
e-mail: info@musicminusone.com